Saber Fencing

for kids:

THAT EVERY PARENT MUST READ

Second Edition

Michael Shender

ISBN-13: 978-1541241985

ISBN-10: 1541241983

DEDICATION

To my Mother. I am sorry, no worldly experience could have prepared you for raising me, but I'm glad you were persistent.

CONTENTS

ACKNOWLEDGMENTS

I wish to thank Coach Alex Fotiyev, Oleh Tretyak, Alex Kushkov, Dr. Leonid Yampolsky and Oleksii Kuznetsov for their support and unparalleled wealth of expertise that they so generously shared, and for their critical and helpful comments on early drafts. I'd like to extend a special thanks to the American Fencing Alliance for raising awareness and making fencing a more popular sport among children. The AFA Roadmap system printed in this book is a compact, clear path for kids to develop fencing skills, leadership qualities, and to stay involved with fencing. I would like to thank my dad for his optimistic support and silly illustrations. Finally, I'd like to thank my sister Nika who has provided an unwavering support in all of my endeavors, and my teammates and friends, Alan, Zach, and Grant, for their friendship and persistent challenge that makes me work harder. I am especially thankful to my mother for introducing me to the sport of fencing and encouraging me every step of my journey.

The Fencing Story

In a land far far away, fencing is the most important sport of all. Fencers gathered from far and wide to compete for glory and medals. So, young Larry and Robin decided to learn the art of fencing. They realized fencers have to be strong, courageous, and disciplined. They must also follow a strict set of rules written in an ancient language that no one can understand. They searched distant lands to find the best master who could teach them this intricate art. To their dismay, they discovered a great

number of fencing schools in lands near and far. They finally set their sights on a great master, who agreed to teach them.

Fencing As An Active Lifestyle

Larry and Robin wanted to learn all they could about fencing and the old book held the best information. The book described fencing as a combat skill, to be used only when your life depended on it. It was necessary to defeat your enemies and protect yourself on the battlefield. The book described acts of bravery and physical fitness, as well as attacks by the sharp point of a blade and cutting edges.

Since then, fencing has become a sport primarily concerned with physical fitness and education. Fencing develops strength, endurance, agility, and personal qualities like determination, courage, self-control, perseverance, and quick thinking.

Fencing is a motorically complex sport imposing high demands on athletes, but is possible to master with constant practice. The complexity of fencing is unparalleled to any other sport. It requires fencers to use all of their physical and mental abilities. Fencers must have agility and fast reaction times to outpace opponents, offensively and defensively.

Fencers must be astute to maintain balance, precise movements,  and exact aim. In addition, fencers must be able to maintain physical performance as well as attention, clarity, and sharpness of mind throughout prolonged tournaments. Research shows that fencing has a far greater impact on brain development than any other sport. Fencer's brains develop more compact and fibrous white matter, which carries signals from one part of the brain to the other. More compact white matter is also associated with faster and more efficient nerve activity.

Important Boring Stuff

Gravity, momentum, and inertia. You've heard about theese even if you are from Mars.

Gravity

You can be certain that if you jump up you will be brought down by gravity. It is important to remember when you practice footwork, the floor is always going to be there to catch you.

Momentum and Inertia

I will not bore you with an explanation about how these are different. An important point to remember is: to start motion you need to apply force.

To change the direction of movement, you need to apply force to stop movement and then apply more force to start a movement in a new direction. The same is true for your opponent.

It is important to remember this when practicing, especially when working on cuts, feints, and footwork.

Geometry

The shortest distance between two points is a straight line. Moving directly forward or backward instead of zigzagging covers more ground, allowing to reach your opponent or get away. Sharp, fast, straight cuts are the most effective.

Larry and Robin worked tirelessly to perfect their footwork, they slashed and thrusted, but still could not win. When sitting at home drinking tea they wondered, "we can run faster than everyone in the class, we can jump higher than everyone in the class, we can do more pushups, and do other exercises better than everyone in the class, but we can't win".

They were brave enough to ask their master, "why can't we win?" The master responded, "It does not only take physical strength to win a fencing match, but also strong knowledge of the rules". He pulled out a dusty book, "this is the guide to fencing written by me and my disciples."

Amazed, Robin and Larry stared at the book. Finally, there it was, fencing explained in a language everyone could understand.

Saber Fencing Simplified

To win, all you have to do is hit your opponent before he hits you, and stay on the strip.

Robin looked at Larry. They were both stunned with confusion. What exactly does that mean? They both wondered. It can't be this easy, can it?

Saber fencing differs from fencing other weapons. Saber fencers may attack using thrusts and cuts with the entire surface of the blade. Saber fencing is exciting and highly maneuverable with fast long movements filled with fast combat actions. The large target makes defensive actions difficult. This makes fencers want to score using <u>active</u> attacking actions, counter-attacks, and fake attacks.

Fencing Strip

Larry and Robin both knew that the strip or piste was a narrow rectangle about six feet wide by about 45 feet long with some lines on it. The strip was for fencing as a court was for basketball. Lines along the long edges of the strip formed side or lateral boundaries. Lines at the ends of the strip were rear boundaries. "Larry, what are the other lines for?" asked Robin. Master told this to Larry earlier. With the pride of knowledge that he now possessed, Larry explained "the two lines closest to the middle are called En Garde lines. Fencers stand behind those before they start fencing. The space between the En Garde lines is often called <u>the box</u>. Lines closer to the back of the strip are warning lines, to tell fencer that they are getting close to the end of the strip." New starting positions, placing saber fencers only three meters apart, are being tested now.

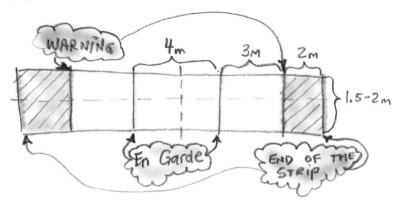

Rules Of The Strip

In the event that a fencer's steps off a strip they are considered to have fallen and unable to score a touch. On the other hand, a fencer that stays on the strip is allowed to score even if the opponent is off the strip. When a fencer steps of the side of a strip the referee will stop fencing. Then fencer who stepped off the strip must move back one meter, about three feet.

"Oh, now I understand" said Larry. "You understand that you can't step off the side of the strip, but what happens if you step off the back of the strip?" Robin said. They turned the page over. Aha! Fencer is allowed to cross the rear boundary, as long as, one foot remains on the strip.

Walk Before You Run

Larry could run faster than any kid in his class, but he could never beat Robin. As it turns out you can't run or walk when you fence saber.

Crossing feet going forward is prohibited. Crossing occurs when back foot completely passes the front foot. Should this occur fencing is stopped and the offender receives a warning - yellow card.

To start moving forward, one must first enter the on guard position. Leading foot in front and another leg behind, with heels on the same line, forming an L-shape. With knees slightly bent. Keep your feet about one and a half of your foot length apart.

Now, you can begin moving forwards or backwards. To move forward move your front leg forward, landing on your heel, then follow it with your back leg. Both legs must move the same distance.

To move backwards you must perform the same action but in reverse. This time you lead with the back leg and follow with the front leg.

A step forward is called ADVANCE, a step back is called RETREAT. Other fencing steps are LUNGE, APPEL, BALESTRA and Flunge were mentioned, but not described. While Robin looked puzzled, impatient Larry thumbed through the book found the entire chapter on footwork a little further.

Another rule stated that a left-handed fencer should always be placed to the left of the referee when facing a right handed opponent.

FOOTWORK

Footwork is the foundation of fencing. Good footwork allows fencers to rapidly accelerate, perform sharp stops, and immediately change directions. Most importantly good footwork allows fencer to stay in balance.

En Garde

This is the starting position, ballet third position is derived from fencing En Garde. To establish the En Garde position fencers place their front foot (right foot if right handed, left if left handed) directly behind the En Garde line. Front foot if positioned along the length of the strip. The heel of the fencers back foot is placed directly behind of the front foot heel. Feet positioned at 90^0 to each other, if brought together they would form an L shape. Move your back foot about one and a half of your foot size back.

After your feet are in position, next you have to square your shoulders to face forward. Place your saber in parry #3 position and bend your knees.
Vous Voilà!

Advance

An advance is a step forward that can be performed in a variety of ways: short, long, slow, and fast. An advance starts with a movement of your <u>front foot forwards</u>, landing on your <u>heel</u>. After landing your front foot finish the advance with a step forward with your back foot. Fencers can vary the size of an advance to create a broken rhythm, and catch their opponents off guard. A series of super short advances (almost in place) is used to prepare an attack while maintaining the right of way.

For instance, you could start your attack with a few short advances and finish the attack with a couple large fast advances.

Retreat

It is arguably the most important skill to master. Anyone can move forwards faster than backwards. Human beings were designed to walk forwards, but not backwards. As a result, it is very difficult to master rapid movements backwards.

You should start a retreat by reaching back with your back foot. After your back foot is placed down, you finish the retreat by bringing your front foot back; the same distance your back foot moved. Retreats can vary in size and speed.

It is important to be able to make a series of rapid retreats. Many fencers lose balance after one or two rapid steps back. To ensure you maintain your balance in a bout, make three or four fast retreat combinations a part of your practice and warm up routine.

Jump Back

Sometimes you must perform a large rapid retreat by jumping back. A jump back is performed by slightly elevating your back leg, then rapidly throwing it further back, while pushing back with the front leg. Finally, this motion is completed by landing both feet simultaneously. A jump back style retreat can be used to perform a fake attack.

Lunge

A lunge is used to end an attack. The size of a lunges depends on how far away your opponent is, and if the opponent is standing still, moving toward you, or away from you.

To lunge from the En Garde position a fencer must elevate their front foot's toes, kick their front foot forwards, push off with their back foot, rapidly extend their saber forwards, and finally land their front foot on the their heel. It is important to check your position at the end of the lunge when practicing.

Looking at the lunge a little closer we notice that lunges can vary in size. In one case you realize that opponent is too close and a quick short lunge is needed to finish your attack spontaneously. In this case a fencer should also finish with a short rapid hand extension; a fencer's arm extension should vary with their lunging distance. In another case, your opponent remained far away. Here, a larger lunge with a strong push from your back leg and a full arm extension is needed, to reach the target.

Image 3.

After a proper lunge, your back foot remains flat on the ground, back leg is straight, and front leg is bent. It is important that your front leg's knee does not pass over the front heel. The angle formed by the front leg should not be less than 90°.

Lunge Exercises

Quarter Game

There are several ways to develop a good lunge. The Quarter game is one of the most effective exercises to develop a correct lunge. To play, place a quarter on the ground and step on it with your heel. In a comfortable En Garde position, lift the toes of your front foot and lunge pushing the quarter forward with your heel. This game will ensure that your front foot is moving parallel to the floor, and most importantly landing on its heel.

Agility Ladder Exercise

For the next routine, you will need an agility ladder. Lay out an agility ladder on the floor. Sit in En Garde position on one side of the ladder with the toes of your front foot against the ladder's edge. Make a half-step into the ladder placing your front foot on its heel inside the square, then lunge over the ladder. Move sideways to face next square and repeat. Making a half step with the heel positions the fencer in wider stance with toes of the front foot pointing up. The biomechanics of this position prevents a common mistake of overloading the front foot and ensuring that final <u>lunge lands on the heel</u>.

Balestra

Also known as a jump step is a very useful technique for keeping balance in the long attack and finishing your attack. It can be performed in place or with a motion forward. The Balestra is performed by a jump while kicking forward with a front foot and landing both feet together. It may sound funny, but it is an effective technique to change rhythms or make an explosive rapid attack. During the balestra There are several biomechanical principles at work. During an advance, fencers are off balance, because they are standing on one leg for a portion of the step. There is only a brief moment between steps when both feet are on the ground. Even then momentum keeps the body off balance. When fencers land after a jump, both feet are firmly planted on the ground, knees are bent and body is in balance this creates a strong foundation for a fast lunge or advance lunge. At the same time, a balestra is a startling move. Your opponent may get scared and run away. Don't worry they can't run too far, but moving further forward unopposed allows you to push your opponent closer to the rear boundary, limiting their options.

Appel

Stomping your front foot on the ground is called an appel. The action looks very similar to an incomplete step forward, or a half advance. An appel is very simple to perform and is useful when performing fake attacks or setting up a counterattack in preparation. For a fake attack, you should practice a combination of a slow advance, sharp appel, retreat or jump back. The counter-attack should start exactly the same way with a slower and softer appel, only replacing jump back with a lunge.

Flunge

This move is a cross breed of fleche and lunge or just a flying lunge. Since crossing feet going forward is not allowed in saber, running attack (fleche - still used in slower foil and epee) was replaced by a rapid flying attack.

The flunge is an advanced step that requires strong balance. It is heavily reliant on core strength and strong legs. Arguably flunge can be even faster than fleche. It is performed by pushing off the front foot rather than back one. Keep in mind fencers that flunge in the box will lose against an opponent performing a regular lunge. DON'T FLUNGE IN THE BOX. Flunge is an athletic move, a failed flunge is almost unrecoverable. Other elements must be perfected before attempting a flunge.

Target Area

The valid saber target area includes head, neck, shoulders, arms above wrists, and body above the line connecting hip bones.

Areas colored red represent valid target area for saber fencers.

Saber Valid Target Area

Although the non-weapon hand is the only unprotected area of a fencer's body, with proper technique the fencer's hand is completely out of your opponent's reach.

Saber - traditionally a cavalry weapon was used while on horseback. In the fight, it was considered ill-mannered to injure a defenseless animal thus limiting target to rider above the saddle.

We can only assume that in those days horses were held in the higher esteem than people riding them.

Saber And How To Hold It

Saber Parts

Saber consists of the following required parts:

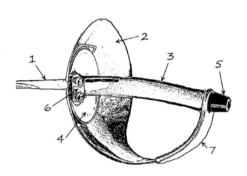

1. Blade
2. Guard
3. Grip
4. Pad
5. Pommel
6. Socket
7. Insulating Sleeve

It is important to note that most of the saber parts are interchangeable for left and right handed fencers except for the guard. Right handed guards are wider on the right, left-handed guards are its mirror image. The socket is installed on the side of the thinner side of the guard.

Holding the saber

To hold the saber place a thumb over the flat area at the top of the grip about half an inch away from the guard, then wrap fingers loosely around the grip.

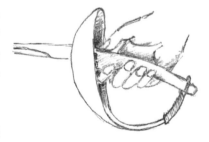

By rotating the wrist and squeezing the grip fencer can perform a number of feints and cuts.

Who scored the touch?

If no rules have been broken and only red light is lit on the scoring box, fencer on the left wins the touch. If there is only a green light lit, fencer on the right wins.

If both red and green lights are on the fencer who has the attack wins. Director decides who had the attack. If both fencers performed identical attacks in the box nobody scores.

When a valid target (anything above the waste except wrists) is touched by a saber the scoring machine turns on a red light for the left fencer and a green light for the right fencer. If both fencers hit simultaneously, both red and green lights will turn on. If one fencer hits just a little bit faster than the other only one light will be on. The second touch will be blocked by the machine. How much is a little bit? 2016 rule change have increased the machine lockout time for saber from 120ms to 170ms. This means that the scoring boxes now are timed to block touches that are 1/6 of a second apart. A little less time than it takes to sneeze.

OH, COOL
WHO IS YOUR MASTER?

The ATTACK mystery

The Word attack has two meanings in fencing. It means priority or a right of way when we talk about who scored. It is also used to describe a type of action or a plan. You will hear names like Quick Attack or Fake Attack.

Attack a.k.a. right of way

Having the attack is the most important aspect of scoring points in fencing. Although scoring points on the attack may seem like a simple task, there are several ways to lose or gain the attack.

To understand if you have the attack, you need to understand what you are doing in relation to the other fencer. One thing is certain you cannot get the attack by standing still. To get the attack you must move forward while extending arm toward the target.

Larry and Robin got on the strip and after command fence they started to charge each other over and over, soon they both got exhausted, neither one of them earned a single point. They wondered why both of them received zero points? When two fencers perform the same action <u>in the box</u> no point is awarded.

Stop

Stop moving forward or move back and your attack is over. Fortunately the same is true for your opponent.

Parry

Parry is a block of the opponent's attack with your sabre. You can gain the attack after a parry by starting your own attack. If you stop or continue moving back you will allow your opponent to start another attack. On the attack, it is important to look-out for the opponent's parry by using feints to confuse your opponent where you are going to hit.

Beat

A beat is a strike on the opponents top ¾ of their blade. This action allows you to gain the attack. While on the offense it is important to look-out for opponents searches to protect your blade from your opponent beats.

Distance Parry

Distance parry is the big name for a dodge. Dodging your opponents hit is an effective way to regain an attack. It is important for an attacker to finish their attack unpredictably to ensure hitting the opponent before they can dodge. Miss the target and your attack is over.

Intricately detailed guards were designed to let fencer break opponent's blade, by catching it in one of the hooks or other openings during the parry.

Riposte

A riposte is an offensive action in response to an opponent's failed attack. For example, Robin starts her attack after Larry falls short, missing his attack. Riposte can be short and immediate, or long requiring a number of steps to reach the retreating opponent. In short riposte is another name for an attack.

The Best Defense Is A Good Offense

Of every 10 points, 8 are scored on the attack. You can dodge and parry all day long, but to score you need to hit the target. Remember, you get no points for hitting the opponents sword. You may only get a point if you hit your opponent. You may be friends off the strip, but on the strip you are competitors. Your competitor has given you permission to hit and will no doubt will not hesitate to hit you to score.

Plan

Most seasoned fencers create a plan before the get En Garde. They decide what action they will perform and what they will do if it fails. Sometimes the plan may have to be revised in action. It is too late to make a plan after the fence command.

For beginner and intermediate fencers their plan mainly consists of deciding what type of attack to perform: quick, long or fake.

Quick Attack

An attack in the box that consists of one or two steps forward and a lunge. This is probably the most frequently performed action in sabre fencing. Frequently quick attacks result in no points awarded to either side. Crazy?! Why waste time and energy on something that gives no points? While it is true that a great number of quick attacks result in no points, it is still one of the most important skills to master.

A well performed quick attack can result in a win, but also it can set the stage to make fake or long attacks more successful.

A quick attack is an effective way to score if your opponent has decided to perform a long attack.

It is a good idea to be prepared for opponents fake attack when your plan is a quick attack. Possible remedies against this crafty move may be: second intention counter-attack, parry, or converting quick attack into a long attack.

Long Attack

A long attack is an attack requiring multiple steps to chase an

OFFENCE

DEFENCE

opponent that is moving backwards. You may use feints to confuse your opponent at the end of this attack. A long attack may require a number of slow preparation steps, followed by several fast steps, and a lunge.

A long attack may be your initial plan if you anticipate that your opponent will move back. A long attack may also be required after a successful fake attack or an opponent's failed attack.

Fake Attack

A fake attack is not an attack at all. A fake attack is an intentional surrender of an attack with such pizzazz and theatrics that forces your opponent to believe that you are performing a quick attack. If performed correctly, your opponent will end their attack too soon and fall short. As result, you regain the attack and advantage over an off-balance opponent.

How to perform these attacks and some useful tips will be discussed after the footwork section.

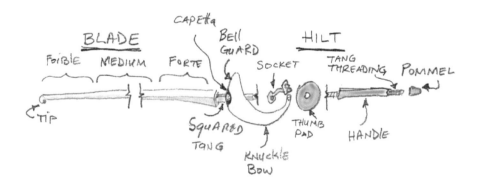

Deconstructed Saber

To Parry Or Not To Parry

Often it is important to be able to block a hit, this is the time for a parry.

Distance Parry

The best parry is simply not being there. Jump back to dodge your opponent's blade and successfully gain the attack by evading your opponent's blade.

Don't guess, know

You must know, not guess the time to move. How would you know when opponent is going to hit, without a mind-reading ability? The answer is simple. MAKE THEM DO IT when you want it. Larry and Robin looked at each other confused. How? Just like a fake attack, a fake counter-attack will do the same trick and force your opponent to swing at you.

Fencing is not reactive, it is proactive. You must force opponents to play your game, to be where you want them to be and do what you want them to do.

Other popular saber parries are 3, 4, 5, and 2. These parries are used to block attacks using the blade. It is important to know and remember parry numbers, so you can follow your fencing master's instructions. Keep in mind the number represents what you are going to protect. For example, parry #3 means that you block the side of the arm that is holding the saber, not your right side, as it is different for righties and lefties.

When learning parries remember X is better than ll.

What to Block not Where to Block

Parry #3

Protects your body on the side of the hand holding the saber. Point the saber straight up in the air. The guard's position is low at waist level. Body and hands are in the En Garde position. During the parry, the wrist of the hand holding the saber pronates outward with a closing motion.

Parry #4

Protects your body on the side opposite of your hand holding the saber. The tip of the saber should point straight up in the air. Keep the guard low and in front at waist level. During the parry, the wrist of the hand holding the saber pronates inward with a closing motion.

Parry #5

Protects the head and shoulders. From En Garde, raise the saber guard directly above your head, holding your saber across with a point slightly higher and forward. Your elbow should not be outside of the vertical line protected by the guard.

#5

#2

Parry #2

Used to block attacks under the arm, cuts, and thrusts to the lower torso. From the En Garde position, point the saber down. It is a more advanced move and not necessarily for beginner fencers.

Circle Parries

Circle #2

Protect multiple sectors with a windshield-wiper like, sweeping motion. Circle parries are a very effective defense tool. During a circle parry, move the point of the saber in a semicircle spiral-like fashion. The end position of the blade determines the parry number. For example, if you start in the En Garde position and during the parry rotate the tip of the saber forward then around drawing an inward spiral ending with the blade down in parry #2 this would make a circle parry 2. In saber, circle parry #3 is probably the most functional. It starts at parry #2 and finishes at parry #3.

Parry, When And How

Saber parries can be done with a motion forwards, at a full stop, or moving back. There is a reason for each type of action. Usually, beginners are taught to take a parry with a step back. This strategy allows more room for error and so is more successful at early stages. Taking a parry at a full stop or moving forward requires additional setup and preparation. These strategies become viable over time, as a fencer develops a sense of distance and timing of the action. All motions need to be timed. There is such thing as too fast. <u>Sometimes fencer must move slowly to prepare the action.</u>

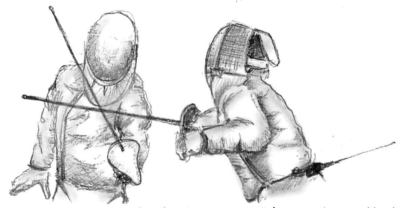

Left-handed fencer (blue) takes parry #4 against an attack of the right-handed fencer (red). Keep in mind the same cut would be called 4 against a lefty and 3 if fencing a righty.

It is advisable to provoke your opponent to hit. This makes your opponent's hit less prepared, more predictable, and easier to parry. There are many ways to provoke your opponent: fake counterattack, search for your opponent's blade, small jump forwards, or simply stop and wait. All of these will do the trick. Keep in mind that your plan is to move back immediately and take a parry.

Known is Good, Unknown not so Much

It is easy to walk with your eyes open. You can easily avoid obstacles and navigate a complex path. With your eyes closed, simple tasks like walking become far more difficult. Cooking with closed eyes is hazardous at best. Crossing a street without looking is deadly.

What do we know?

- We know that attackers are looking for an opportunity to finish the attack with a cut or a thrust, as soon as you give them an opening.
- We know that your opponent's saber is the same length as yours.
- We know that attackers will not attempt to hit when they are too far away.
- We know that attackers need to continuously move forwards.
- We know if your opponent is right handed or left handed.
- We know that attackers feel confident when you are almost off the strip and unable to move further back.
- We know that holding your saber with the tip pointing forward will make it more challenging for an attacker to get close.
- We know that the shortest distance between two points is a straight line.
- We know that a taller opponent is more likely to hit your upper regions, head, and shoulders
- We know that a shorter opponent is more likely to hit your lower regions, under-arm, and to thrust.
- We know the current position of your opponent's saber.

- We know where the previous attacks landed, also we know what actions the opponent favors by observing other bouts.
- We may also know what actions the referee may favor.

Only knowledge relevant to the current bout is useful knowledge.

- We also know if it's warm or cold outside, if you have unfinished homework, if somebody is screaming on the adjacent strip, if your parents are watching, where you will go for dinner, what you will eat for dinner, and $E=MC^2$. This is not useful in the bout, ignore it.

Using the useful knowledge, we can formulate a defense strategy. You know that the attacker needs to finish the attack, even if both light go off, the attacker wins. If attackers see a counterattack coming, they will attempt to hit as quickly as possible to score. This is why using a fake counter-attack is a good idea. Now that you have successfully provoked your opponent to finish their attack prematurely, you must decide what parry to take and how. When an attacker believes that a counter attack is imminent, they don't have time for complex blade movements and are forced to finish the attack quickly to the sector where the blade is pointing.

With a shorter opponent, you may choose to take a distance parry. With distance parry, the attackers will miss no matter where they try to hit. So, immediately following the fake counterattack you must jump back and take one additional step back to dodge. It is also a good idea to take a parry while you are jumping back. It will protect you if you did not move far enough. For beginners, parry #3 or circle parry #3 are good ideas.

If your opponent has the tip of their saber up, following a fake counterattack you may choose to jump back and take parry #5. More advanced fencers may choose to step forward following a fake counterattack and take parry #5 with a rapid riposte. This move, if done properly, limits when and where your opponent can hit so severely that they will have a hard time avoiding your parry. Parry #2 or #3 are smart choices if the attacker's blade is pointing down.

Searches and Invitations

Other Ways to provoke attackers are searches and invitations.

Search

You may choose to beat the attackers' blade to gain the attack. You must rotate your saber in a circular motion to find the attackers' blade. <u>Not every search is successful</u> and usually presents an opportunity for the attacker to score. Knowing this, you may use the search as a provocation and immediately cover exposed area. Using the same strategy as before, you may take parry #3 or #5 if attacker's blade is up or parry #3 or #2 if attacker's blade is down.

Invitation

Simply expose the area that you want your opponent to hit and then parry the attack to that area. For example, you may move your saber to a position in the middle, exposing your hand, then take parry #3 if the attacker takes the bait. Keep in mind, a smart attacker will pretend to fall into your trap and will <u>faint</u> (fake) to your exposed area then hit a different location. In this case, an attacker might faint 3 then attack 4. This is why you need to perfect timing and style of invitations.

All these tricks will not work every time, but they will improve your odds. For example, if you decide to hold parry #5, you will be exposing areas 3 and 4. When your opponent makes a cut, take parry #4. Your odds of success are 50/50. If you score on every two out of three of your attacks and your defensive game is 50/50 you win the bout, but you can do even better.

Stop guessing. Anticipate!

If you stop guessing and anticipate the attack you improve your odds substantially. You start by counting how many times your opponents attacks 3, 4 and 5. They will not be able to resist when you invite them to attack their favorite spot. You should be able to easily parry anticipated attacks.

Don't Take A Parry Early

Your opponent can see an early parry and change the direction of  their attack. On the other hand if you see your opponent is ready to strike, you can perform an invitation and take a fake parry just a bit early, exposing where you want them to hit, then move to actual parry. Outsmarting your opponent is one of the most enjoyable parts of the game.

The ancient question of TIME and SPACE

 By now your head is probably spinning trying to visualize all this parry stuff. It is filled with questions of where do I stand and how do I move. I will be honest, this book may give you a better understanding of fencing, but you would have to buy fairy dust that instantaneously makes you a wonder fencer from another merchant.

You have to practice, practice, practice and when you're done practicing, practice some more to become great.

These techniques will work perfectly only after you master timing and distance. It is very important to understand the distance between you and your opponent that is needed to successfully trick them into believing your counterattack is real. At the same time, you have to gauge how far you have to be to get clear of their attack once it comes. You need to develop body language and theatrics that make your fake intentions convincing.

Use A Parry To Set Up A Counterattack

Moving your hand into a parry position can be used to prepare a counterattack. The attacker may get confused and hesitate just a bit if you suddenly take several parries. This may create an opening for a counterattack. For example, rapidly take parry #4 then #5, counterattack by flicking to your opponent's 3 (forearm) and jump back taking parry #3 or #5.

COMPETITIVE FENCING

ATTACK

The fencing rule book defines an attack as: "The initial offensive action made by extending the arm and continuously threatening the opponent's target …"

This is a vague definition. Many referees are confused by it and their interpretations differ from one to the other. It is important to remember that directors are human, they do their best to interpret your fast-paced actions, usually without video replay at their disposal.

Attack In The Box

It is important to highlight this one attack scenario in particular. It is probably the most frequently performed action in saber fencing. The attack in the box occurs immediately after the "fence" command is given. If both fencers charge forward and touch valid target at the same time, both lights register on the machine. One fencer may win and the other loses. Why is that?

A few elements which fencers should pay particular attention to:

1. Footwork.

    Many referees will look for aggressive footwork, constant motion forward and ending of the attack with a lunge.

    If the footwork of both fencers is symmetrical, the call may be made based on blade and hand motion.

2. Hand motion.

If both fencers have symmetrical footwork, the fencer who begins the hand extension first while IN DISTANCE wins over a fencer who hesitates. Extending your hand out of distance will result in losing the attack. Many define the right distance or IN DISTANCE as close enough to reach your opponent with a lunge or one step and hand extension.

3. Blade position.

If footwork and hand position are the same, blade position decides the attack. A blade pointing forward towards the target wins over a blade pointing away from it. Be careful not to swing during the final cut as it can the change direction of the blade to point away from the target, causing loss of the attack.

C-   A+

4. Line of attack

Lastly, a fencer who performs a straight attack in one line wins over a fencers who performs feints or searches before the final cut.

5. Director

Pay particular attention to actions favored by the director. As you understand by now, all fencing actions are scored based on the rule interpreted by a human. However, there is a small problem with humans, they are all different. Different vision, reactions, vantage points, personal fencing backgrounds, endurance, and other factors can affect a director's calls. If you disagree with a call, POLITELY ask why this call was made and listen carefully. Referees will look for footwork, blade position, hand extension, and line of the attack. Adjust your game according to the referee's previous calls.

The attack in the box can be done with a single advance and lunge or a double advance and lunge. The size of the advance and lunge can vary to outplay your opponent. You can make your opponent hesitate or end their attack too soon. For example, a single small or medium sized advance followed by a rapid lunge may catch your opponent in preparation.

Long Attack with Feints

Attacks that have multiple steps to reach your opponent are referred to as long attacks. An attack with multiple movements of the blade, beats, and feints is called a composite attack. To perform an effective long attack, you should make several blade motions paired with complex footwork.

Although there are an infinite number of combinations of footwork and blade movements, it is important to split the attack into two parts: slow preparation and fast finish. Let's consider a common long attack: triple advance, double advance, ballestra lunge. The preparation would be the triple advance and should be performed slowly. Next comes the explosive finish with a double advance, balestra, lunge. Do not forget to include feints throughout the long attack and when finishing. Beginner fencers should pick a target during the preparatory phase, this will remove hesitation when finishing.

Fake Attack

A fake attack is also called an in and out. To perform this action you must first give up the attack in such a way that opponent is likely to fail immediately after.

I know it's a bit confusing. Let's clarify. Both fencers perform simultaneous attacks in the box one after another, with no points scored. Larry decides to trick Robin into believing that he is going

to do another quick attack in the box, but instead he stops sharply and moves back as Robin completes her advance and lunge attack, falling short and missing the target. After Robin failed her attack, Larry regains the attack and an opportunity to score a riposte on Robin who is not able to move back immediately after the lunge.

Larry decided to do a fake attack and Robin committed to performing a quick attack. Larry sharply changed direction when fooled Robin lunged too early.

Robin lost her attack after she fell short and missed. Larry started moving forward preparing his attack.

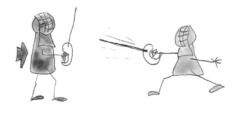

Point-in-line

It is important to mention a technique called point-in-line. It is important to recognize point-in-line and know what to do if this technique is used against you. Point-in-line is not recommended to be used by beginners. There are many alternative uses for point-in-line, like setting up various counter-attacks and parries. In fact, a separate book can be written just about point-in-line.

What is a point-in-line? Point-in-line is a tactical priority or the right of way, A.K.A. the attack. A fencer that establishes point-in-line immediately takes over the attack. Once point-in-line is broken, the attack is lost.

How is point-in-line is established?
Point-in-line is a position in which the fencer's sword arm is kept straight, forming a continuous line with the blade, the saber guard is turned outward, and the point continually threatens the opponent's valid target. Point-in-line must be established

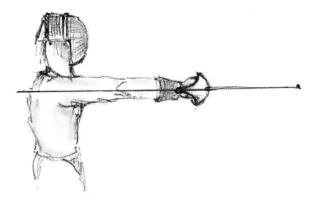

off distance. This means that the fencer establishing it must increase distance with the opponent. The saber point must be aimed directly at the high lines of the target for the point-in-line to remain intact.

What breaks point-in-line?
The following actions will break point-in-line: bending your wrist or elbow, or moving point outside of the opponent's target area. Unfortunately, point-in-line rules are vague and as result, referees are not consistent. As it stands today, to maintain point-in-line the fencer is allowed only one disengage, advance or lunge. Moving forward more than that, twirling, or twisting the saber guard down breaks point-in-line. Blade contact with opponents' saber also breaks point-in-line.

How to score?
When both fencers hit together, only the attacker scores. The fencer holding point-in-line has the attack, but the touch can only be scored with the point. In other words, to score with point-in-line you must thrust your saber into your opponent while maintaining point-in-line intact. If a touch is made with any other part of the blade, then you can win the point only if your opponent misses or does not hit in time. This touch would be considered a counter-attack.

Private Lessons

Private lessons are an important part of learning to fence. Working with a coach one-on-one fine tunes a fencer's technique through personalized instruction. Since half a second can be the difference between winning and losing a touch, it is very important to perfect every aspect of a fencer's body and blade movements. Attention to detail saves the proper movements to muscle memory and allows students to continue practicing them in group lessons and free fencing. As a result, the great attention placed on an individual's learning curve tends to bring faster results than group lessons alone.

Private lessons usually involve a more disciplined approach to coaching, which produces visible results faster. Coaches hold their students to higher degrees of accountability. Students learn to arrive to their lessons on time and warm up beforehand. They exercise, stretch, and wait for their coach with their weapon and mask in hand, developing great time management skills. Since learning to properly warm up your body before fencing is a necessary skill for competitions, private lessons teach students the individual accountability necessary to mentally and physically prepare for a  tournament. During the lesson, coaches also get to know a fencer's strengths and weaknesses and are able to give them better advice, during group lessons and competitions. The rapport developed during a private lesson translates into more targeted coaching in other areas of training, building an amazing foundation for future learning.

Tournament First Timers

Larry and Robin decided to go to a tournament, but they knew very little about them. They were very worried that they were not prepared. They had a lot of questions about what equipment was need, where they should go, and how the score is kept?

What to bring checklist

The rules require that fencers must have the following items:

- Tall Socks (covering any part of the leg not covered by pants)
- Knickers (fencing pants)
- Underarm protector (½ jacket)
- Fencing Jacket
- Plastic chest protector
          (Optional for men, mandatory for female fencers)
- Saber Mask
- Lame
- Saber glove
- 2 body cords
- 2 mask cords
- 2 sabers

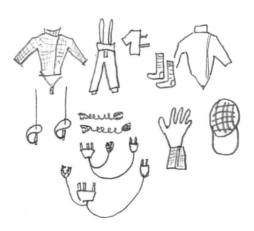

Equipment Inspection

At larger tournaments, your equipment may be required to pass an inspection. Inspectors will check your equipment and mark it with inspection marks that will be checked later by directors.

Visual inspection

An inspector or bout director will check to see that your equipment has no holes, cracks, or tears. Your mask may also be subjected to a punch test to make sure it is safe. Time-to-time you should inspect your own equipment yourself to make sure it's up to regulation.

Electric Equipment Testing

Electric testing is performed for all electric equipment, usually with the exception of the saber. Your lame, glove, and mask are tested and marked with stamps. All cords are also tested and marked with colored tape. Tape from prior inspections should be removed prior to the next tournament.

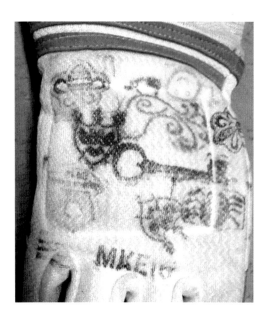

Individual Tournament

In a tournament with many people, fencers are first separated in groups called pools. These pools usually have five to seven fencers. Competitors fence five touch bouts with everyone in their pool. Based on the results of pool bouts, fencers are seeded into a direct elimination table. They fence Direct Elimination (DE) bouts until only the winner remains.

For example, a pool table may look something like this:

POOL 1

	Fencer	1	2	3		VI	TS	TR	TI	Place
1	Larry		V	4		1	9	7	2	1
2	Robin	2		V		1	7	6	1	2
3	Jim	V	1			1	6	9	-3	3

1 vs 2 1-YC CROSSED		2 vs 3	1 vs 3

Translation

VI - Victory Indicator.
VI - primary and the most important performance measure.
Victory Indicator shows a number of bouts won by fencer in the pool round.

TS - Touches Scored (add all points in the fencer's row)
TR - Touches Received (add all points in the fencer's column)

Touch Indicator - TI

TI - is secondary, but also an extremely important measure. Touch Indicator is calculated by subtracting TR from TS i.e. touches scored minus touches received. It is used as a tiebreaker for fencers with an equal number of victories.

V - Victory

Pool bouts are fenced to 5 touches, so V = 5 points. In some cases one can win with less than 5 points. For example, to record a victory with 3 points scored the director would write V3, this can occur when fencers run out of time in a bout.

If the number of victories are tied among multiple fencers, then the TI determines placement. Below the table there is usually a bout order. Directors will cross out bouts that already took place and must record any violations on the score sheet. You can see that fencer 1 (Larry) received a Yellow Card for crossing.

Ordinarily, six fencers would not be split into two pools. However, to illustrate a tournament with multiple pools, we split competitors into two pools of three.

POOL 2

	Fencer	1	2	3	VI	TS	TR	TI	Place
1	Mims		1	4	0	5	10	-5	3
2	Nia	V		V	2	10	2	8	1
3	Sammy	V	2		1	7	9	-2	2

Seeding After Pools

Place	Fencer	VI	TI
1	Nia	2	8
2	Larry	1	2
3	Robin	1	1
4	Sammy	1	-2
5	Jim	1	-3
6	Mims	0	-5
7	-		
8	-		

DE Tableau

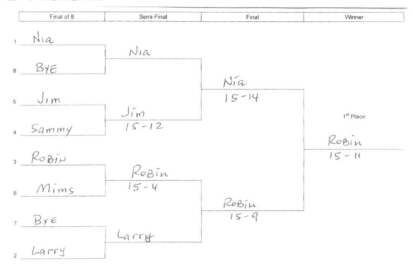

Final of 8	Semi-Final	Final	Winner

1. Nia
8. BYE

Nia

5. Jim
4. Sammy

Jim
15-12

3. RoBiN
6. Mims

RoBiN
15-4

7. ByE
2. Larry

Larry

Nia
15-14

RoBiN
15-9

1st Place

RoBiN
15-11

Who is Bye?

The DE table is filled to make an even number of fencers based on the following progression: 2, 4, 8, 16, 32, 64 .... Fencers are placed in the DE Tableau is based on their performance in the pools: First vs Last, Second vs. Second to Last, etc. In this case 1st and 2nd ranked fencers out of pools have nobody to fence since there is no 7th and 8th fencer. 1 and 2 get a <u>Bye</u> and advance to the next round unopposed.

Each bout's score is recorded under the winner's name.

Final results

Place	Fencer
1	Robin
2	Nia
3T	Larry
3T	Jim
5	Sammy
6	Mims

Robin won 1st place, defeating Nia with a score of 15-11 in the final bout.

Larry and Jim are tied for 3rd place, because there was no fence-off for third in this tournament.

The tournament format is important.
This tournament had a 100% promotion to DE after pools. Some of the larger tournaments have 80% promotion to DE. This means that only the top 80% of fencers will advance to the DE round.

Oops?!

Team Match

Team matches are usually fenced as a relay to 45 touches. The strongest fencer usually anchors the relay.

Team A						Team B		
1	Robin			vs		Mims		4
2	Larry					Nia		5
3	Jim					Sammy		6
#	Fencer	Touches	Score		Score	Touches	Fencer	#
3	Jim	5	5		1	1	Sammy	6
1	Robin	5	10		9	8	Nia	5
2	Larry	5	15		11	2	Mims	4
1	Robin	5	20		14	3	Sammy	6
3	Jim	5	25		14	0	Mims	4
2	Larry	5	30		28	14	Nia	5
1	Robin	5	35		31	3	Mims	4
2	Larry	5	40		33	2	Sammy	6
3	Jim	3	43		45	12	Nia	5
Penalties			Final Score		Final Score	Penalties		
3 - YC crossing 3 - RC disobedience			43		45	4 - YC turning during bout		

Penalties

Fencers receive penalties for breaking rules. There are four types of penalties.

1. Ground penalty

This penalty is given if a fencer steps off the strip during fencing. The penalized fencer must move back one meter.

2. Yellow card

This penalty is given to the fencer for the <u>first offense</u>. No points is awarded to the opponent, and then touch is annulled (does not count). This penalty may result in a loss of a point if both fencers hit.

For example, Larry is performing an attack and Robin counterattacks. Larry crossed his feet as both fencers hit. With both lights on Larry receives a yellow card. Larry's touch is annulled while Robin's touch is good. Robin wins this point.

Spectators and coaches can also receive a yellow card as warning for disturbances. For them, second offense results in the black card.

3. Red Card

This penalty is given if the offense is severe or for every subsequent yellow card offense. For example Larry receives a yellow card for crossing feet, every time he crosses his feet again, in the same bout, he will receive a red card.

If no penalties of any kind are given and Larry receives a yellow or red card, then every penalty that would otherwise resulted in a yellow card will cause a red card and a point awarded to his opponent. Using an earlier example, Larry receives a yellow card for crossing his feet during his attack as Robin counterattacks. The score is 1 - Robin, 0 - Larry.

The same thing happens again. Larry now receives a red card. Robin gets two points. One for the valid touch and another for Larry's red card. The score is now is 3 - Robin, 0 - Larry.

After the fence command during his first step Larry crosses feet again going forward, but fencers do not yet hit. The referee will yell halt and Larry will receive a red card. The score becomes 4 - Robin, 0 - Larry.

4. Black Card

This is the most severe form of punishment. This card is given mostly for disciplinary offenses and cheating, offenders are disqualified from the competition. Spectators and coaches can also receive a black card.

Another way to look at penalties is by group. There are four groups of penalties:

Penalty Groups

- 1st Group
  Generally offenses in this group are penalized with a yellow card for their first offense.

- 2nd Group
  Offenses in this group are penalized with a red card.

- 3rd Group
  Fencers will get a red card for their first offense in this group and a black card for their second offense.

- 4th Group
  A black card is given for all offenses in this group.

A complete list of penalties can be found online, but here is a list of a few easily avoidable penalties.

Offense	1st	2nd	3rd
Fencer not present	1st Call	2nd Call	3rd Call
Turning the back to the opponent			
Touching electrical equipment			
Covering target			
Disobeying the referee			
Taking mask off before Halt			
Using non-weapon arm or hand			
Disturbing order on the strip			
Deliberate Brutality			

Mind Over Matter

Paralyzing fear, nerves, heart skipping a beat, and butterflies in your stomach are all performance killing effects of your brain's chemistry. People are hardwired to experience fear as self-preservation safeguard that stops them from doing something dangerous. Everybody gets nervous and scared. Good news! There are ways to get less nervous.

Another important point to consider is that people have limits on how fast they run, how high they jump, and how much information they can process in a second. It turns out we can process huge amounts of data very fast. Our eyes, ears, nose, hands, feet can constantly capture data. We also have amazing capability for parallel processing, like walking and chewing bubble gum at the same time, but everything has its limits. Every added simultaneous task slows other processes down. We would have a harder time doing math while watching TV and running on a treadmill. Focusing on one task is a skill.

A good fencer is able to tune out all outside noise and focus on the bout.

Kill The Fear

So, first of all, let me assert my firm belief that the only thing we have to fear is fear itself — nameless, unreasoning, unjustified terror which paralyzes needed efforts to convert retreat into advance.

Franklin D. Roosevelt

Beginner's luck is a paradigm that occurs due to very low initial expectations. First timers usually score points and sometimes even win bouts because they are less afraid to loose. Often, you can clearly see a moment when a fencer becomes tense, movements become jagged and slow as fear of loss overloads the brain.

Is it even possible to change natural brain chemistry and body response? The simple answer is YES.

There are many things you can do to avoid and manage fear before and during tournaments. The following are few of them:

1. Routine
2. Physical exercise
3. Ritual
4. Visualization

Routine

Development of a good routine helps to reduce chaos and remain focused on a task. Create a checklist and agenda of what you need to bring, where you need to be, and at what times. The night before lay out clothing you will wear the following day, in order of what goes on last on the bottom and first on the top. Decide where you go for breakfast and what you will have. This sounds excessive, but it removes uncertainty and unnecessary stress from what is already stressful day.

Make sure there is time to warm up, stretch, dress, and fence warm-up bouts.

Sample checklist may be as follows:

☐	Chest protector	6:30 am	Wake up
☐	Plastron	7:00 am	Breakfast place, pancakes
☐	Socks	8:00 am	Equipment check
☐	Knickers	8:20 am	Buy saber
☐	Jacket	8:30 am	Check-in
☐	Lame	9:00 am	Warm-up
☐	Glove	9:15 am	Dress
☐	Mask	9:20 am	Fence warm-up bouts
☐	Sneakers	9:40 am	Visualization
☐	Sabers	9:45 am	Check-in Closed, find your strip
☐	Body Cords	9:50 am	At your strip with equipment
☐	Mask Cords		ready to win
☐	Headphones		
☐	Phone		
☐	Snack		
☐	Journal		
☐	Passport or ID		

Physical exercise

It makes people happy, because physical exercise induces the release of endorphins. Endorphins are chemicals that promote happiness. Your warm-up routine has to be intensive enough to wake up your muscles and release endorphins, yet leave enough energy for competition. Make sure you approach your warm-up routine systematically. You may choose to use the following template for your top to bottom warm up:

All exercises should start slow, gradually increasing in range of motion. Consider doing ten repetitions or so for each one of the points below.

1. Tune out distractions with the up-tempo music.
2. Start with walking, slowly increasing pace.
3. As you walk, slow circles with your head clockwise and counterclockwise.
4. Shoulder circles forward and back.
5. Hands big circles forward, then back.
6. Right hand up, left down, switch hand positions with every step.
7. Bend forward and touch front foot with every step.
8. Touch opposite foot with every step.
9. Slow jogging.
10. Side step with right then left shoulder forward.
11. Jogging almost in place with High knees.
12. Jogging almost in place with High Heels.
13. Torso rotations right and left.
14. Stretch fingers, hands, shoulders
15. Stretch Leg muscles
16. Footwork
    i) advances slow then fast
    ii) retreats slow then fast
    iii) lunge, slowly increasing in speed and range
    iv) combinations such as:
        (1) advance lunge
        (2) ballestra advance lunge
        (3) advance, appel, jump back, advance, lunge.
        (4) double retreat, advance, lunge
17. Get dressed for fencing, fence warm-up starting slowly, and gradually increasing in intensity. Keep in mind you are not trying to win yet. This is just a warm up.

Rituals

Rituals help conquer fear. Pump yourself up. Ritualistic dances were used by tribes to set warriors in the fighting mood.

We don't suggest humming and dancing in circles on the strip, but something more subtle is appropriate.

Frequently people are most anxious right before an activity.

Let's imagine you have to parachute out of a plane for the first time. You are very scared, but you will only jump when you are prepared. Prepare yourself before the start of a bout, so you can fence without fear.

If you come En Garde when you are nervous, the referee will call fence before you've taken hold of your emotions and you are likely to lose. Get your emotions under control before you get to En Garde.

En Garde ritual:

Take a slow deep breath in through your nose, short pause, let it out through your mouth, and take another after a short pause. Breath normally. Put your front foot against the En Garde line. Move your back foot into a comfortable position. Slow deep breath in through your nose, short pause, let it out through your mouth, short pause. Breath normal. Bend your knees, raise your weapon only when completely ready.

Lost Point ritual:

Don't rush back after you lose a point. Break the rhythm, walk towards back of the strip, fix your glove, straighten your weapon. Don't focus on breaking the rhythm, focus on the strategy for your next point.

Need a break rituals:

Fencers are not allowed to take time to rest during the bout, however with permission of the referee they are allowed to take a little bit of time to fix and adjust things like:

- Fix hair.
- Fix lining of the mask.
- Pull up socks
- Straighten the weapon.
- Tie shoelaces tighter.

This is not going to buy you a lot of time, but it may be enough to catch a breath and re-focus.

Visualization

Children learn by imitating actions of adults. They see body movement and try to repeat it, with help of a more experienced individual they perfect it. When you simply imagine doing something, your brain activates many of the neural networks and cell connections as if you actually did it. If you frequently imagine performing a task, you condition your neural pathways so that the task seems familiar when you actually do it. This trains the brain and forms synapse  connections. Visualize every step of the task, every small detail. This helps keep focus away from fear. There are numerous visualization techniques specifically designed to deal with fear.

Bunny turns dragon, dragon turns bunny

Often when two evenly matched competitors meet, one still wins and another loses. The loser then becomes a bunny and the winner becomes a dragon.

Many fencers lose before the competition even begins. They look at who is in front of them and make their mind up based on thinking "I always lose to him/her, this kid is so good, a winner of the last tournament…" in doing so they become a bunny. On the other side of the room the dragon is growing more confident by saying "I always win against these fencers".

It is important to reinforce bunnies, encourage them and emphasize every success against their dragons, even if this success belongs to someone else. Let's say the dragon lost to another that kid bunny once beat.

Nobody is unbeatable

At the same time it is important for the dragon not to underestimate bunny. Bunny has been practicing, the tables can turn and the dragon will become a bunny.

PARENTAL CAUTION! Unless you fence yourself, kids will not take your advice seriously. The wealth of knowledge you have accumulated is important, but ineffective when you are not perceived by your kid as not a fencing expert. Don't let them offend you and don't take offense. You are part of the team, not just a driver. Let them know that you hold their side and support them like no one else.

Roadmap

American Fencing Alliance has developed a skills chart to serve as a goal-oriented roadmap for young fencers. It clearly marks a path of learning, timing, and perfecting of particular skills.

Fencer must learn and demonstrate proficiency in the following areas:
1. Footwork
2. Bladework
3. Etiquette
4. Rules
5. Practical application of 1, 2, 3, 4 in a bout

Skills Scale by Level:
1. Knows the concept (10%)
2. Knows and understands the concept (20%)
3. Able to execute rarely (30%)
4. Able to execute sometimes (40%)
5. Able to execute 50% of the times
6. Able to execute often (60%0
7. Able to execute very often (70%)
8. Able to execute most of the times (80%)
9. Able to execute most of the times with confidence (90%)
10. Able to execute nearly flawlessly (100%)

This envisioned a four-year program. The exact duration will depend on each individual's involvement and ability.

Year 1 (Month 0 - 10)
Year 2 (Month 12 - 20)
Year 3 (Month 22 - 30)
Year 4 (Month 30 - 36)

First Year

Month	Classification	Saber Skills	Passing
2	Apprentice	Advance, Retreat, Double A/R, Lunge	80%
		En Garde position, Parry 3, 4, 5 (or any 3 parries)	50%
		Fence 1-5 touch bout, knowledge of bout rules and etiquette	70%
4	Basic I	Advance, Retreat, Double A/R, Lunge, Appel Lunge,	80%
		Quick Attack, Fake Attack	50%
		En Garde position, Parry 3, 4, 5 (or any 3 parries)	70%
		Fence 1-5 touch bout, knowledge of bout rules and etiquette	80%
6	Basic II	Advance, Retreat, Double A/R, Lunge, Appel Lunge,	80%
		Quick Attack, Fake Attack	60%
		En Garde position, Parry 3, 4, 5 (or any 3 parries)	80%
		Fence 1-5 touch bout, knowledge of bout rules and etiquette	90%
8	Basic III	Advance, Retreat, Double A/R, Lunge, Appel Lunge,	80%
		Quick Attack, Fake Attack	70%
		En Garde position, Parry 3, 4, 5 (or any 3 parries)	90%
		Fence 1-5 touch bout, knowledge of bout rules and etiquette	100%
10	Musketeer I	Advance, Retreat, Double A/R, Lunge, Appel Lunge, Balestra	80%
		Quick Attack, Fake Attack, Long Attack	50%
		En Garde position, Parry 2, 3, 4, 5 (or any 4 parries)	90%
		Referee bout	30%
		Fence Pools and DE, display proper attitude	Win 1

Second Year

Month	Classification	Saber Skills	Passing
12	Musketeer II	Advance, Retreat, Double A/R, Lunge, Appel Lunge, Balestra	80%
		Quick Attack, Fake Attack, Long Attack	60%
		En Garde position, Parry 2, 3, 4, 5 (or any 4 parries)	90%
		Referee bout	30%
		Fence Pools and DE, display proper attitude	Win 1
14	Musketeer III	Advance, Retreat, Double A/R, Lunge, Appel Lunge, Balestra	80%
		Quick Attack, Fake Attack, Long Attack	70%
		En Garde position, Parry 2, 3, 4, 5 (or any 4 parries)	90%
		Referee bout	30%
		Fence Pools and DE, display proper attitude	Win 1
16	Pirate I	Advance, Retreat, Double A/R, Lunge, Appel Lunge, Balestra Lunge	80%
		Quick Attack, Fake Attack, Long Attack, Beat attack/defense	70%
		En Garde position, Parry 2, 3, 4, 5 (or any 4 parries)	100%
		Referee bout	40%
		Fence Pools and DE, display proper attitude	Win 2
18	Pirate II	Advance, Retreat, Double A/R, Lunge, Appel Lunge, Balestra Lunge	80%
		Quick Attack, Fake Attack, Long Attack, Beat attack/defense	80%
		En Garde position, Parry 2, 3, 4, 5 (or any 4 parries)	100%
		Referee bout	40%
		Fence Pools and DE, display proper attitude	Win 2
20	Pirate III	Advance, Retreat, Double A/R, Lunge, Appel Lunge, Balestra Lunge	80%
		Quick Attack, Fake Attack, Long Attack, Beat attack/defense	90%
		En Garde position, Parry 2, 3, 4, 5 (or any 4 parries)	100%
		Referee bout	40%
		Fence Pools and DE, display proper attitude	Win 2

Third Year

Month	Classification	Saber Skills	Passing
22	Duelist I	Advance, Retreat, Double A/R + L, Appel Lunge, Balestra A/L	80%
		Attack (Quick, Fake, Long), Beat attack/defense, Feints	70%
		Parry 2, 3, 4, 5, Circle 3/4 (or any 6 parries)	70%
		Advanced concepts: invitation, second intention	10%
		Referee bout	50%
		Fence Pools and DE, display proper attitude	Pass 1 Round
24	Duelist II	Advance, Retreat, Double A/R + L, Appel Lunge, Balestra A/L	80%
		Attack (Quick, Fake, Long), Beat attack/defense, Feints	80%
		Parry 2, 3, 4, 5, Circle 3/4 (or any 6 parries)	80%
		Advanced concepts: invitation, second intention	30%
		Referee bout	50%
		Fence Pools and DE, display proper attitude	Pass 1 Round
26	Duelist III	Advance, Retreat, Double A/R + L, Appel Lunge, Balestra A/L	80%
		Attack (Quick, Fake, Long), Beat attack/defense, Feints	90%
		Parry 2, 3, 4, 5, Circle 3/4 (or any 6 parries)	100%
		Advanced concepts: invitation, second intention	50%
		Referee bout	50%
		Fence Pools and DE, display proper attitude	Pass 1 Round

28	Competitor I	Advance, Retreat, Double A/R + L, Appel Lunge, Balestra A/L	90%
		Attack (Quick, Fake, Long), Beat attack/defense, Feints	80%
		Parry 2, 3, 4, 5, Circle 3/4/5 (or any 7 parries),	80%
		Advanced concepts: invitation, second intention	60%
		Referee bout	60%
		Fence Pools, DE, and teams, display proper attitude	Pass 2 Rounds
30	Competitor II	Advance, Retreat, Double A/R + L, Appel Lunge, Balestra A/L	95%
		Attack (Quick, Fake, Long), Beat attack/defense, Feints	90%
		Parry 2, 3, 4, 5, Circle 3/4/5 (or any 7 parries)	80%
		Advanced concepts: invitation, second intention	70%
		Referee bout	70%
		Fence Pools, DE, teams, proper attitude, provide support to teammates	Pass 2 Rounds

Fourth Year

Month	Classification	Saber Skills	Passing
32	Competitor III	Advance, Retreat, Double A/R + L, Appel Lunge, Balestra A/L	100%
		Attack (Quick, Fake, Long), Beat attack/defense, Feints	90%
		Advanced concepts: invitation, second intention	80%
		Parry 2, 3, 4, 5, Circle 3/4/5 (or any 7 parries)	100%
		Referee bout	80%
		Fence Pools, DE, teams, proper attitude, support and organize the team	Pass 2 Rounds
34	Captain	Advance, Retreat, Double A/R, Lunge, Appel Lunge, Balestra A/L	100%
		Attacks: straight, compound, fake, feints	100%
		Defense: Beat attack/defense, Point-in-line,	100%
		Flunge, stop-cut, pris de fer	90%
		Advanced concepts: invitation, second intention	90%
		Parry 2, 3, 4, 5, Circle 3/4/5 (or any 7 parries)	100%
		Referee bout	80%
		Fence Pools, DE, teams, proper attitude, support and organize the team	Final 4 of 9 or more
36	Team Captain	Advance, Retreat, Double A/R, Lunge, Appel Lunge, Balestra A/L	100%
		Attacks: straight, compound, fake, feints	100%
		Defense: Beat attack/defense, Point-in-line,	100%
		Advanced concepts: invitation, second intention	100%
		Flunge, stop-cut, pris de fer	100%
		Parry 2, 3, 4, 5, Circle 3/4/5 (or any 7 parries)	100%
		Referee bout	90%
		Fence Pools, DE, teams, proper attitude, support and organize the team	1st of 9 or more

There is no substitute for skill.
Practice often. Practice hard.

There is not a single fencer in the world that has never lost. Don't get discouraged by losses, simply practice harder. Don't expect to win and continue winning, your opponents have been practicing. Practice more, and you will become a success.

If at first you don't succeed,
Try, try, try again.

W. E. Hickson

Made in the USA
Coppell, TX
02 March 2022

74308494R00048